73

Yesterday Won't Goodbye

Yesterday Won't Goodbye
a collection of poetry

cx

by Brian Ellis

Write Bloody Publishing
America's Independent Press

Long Beach, CA

writebloody.com

Ellis, Brian.
1st edition.
ISBN: 978-1-935904-12-0

Interior Layout by Lea C. Deschenes
Cover Designed by Joshua Grieve
Proofread and Edited by Sarah Kay and Jennifer Roach
Type set in Aller and Bergamo: www.theleagueofmoveabletype.com

Printed in Tennessee, USA

Write Bloody Publishing
Long Beach, CA
Support Independent Presses
writebloody.com

To contact the author, send an email to writebloody@gmail.com

YESTERDAY WON'T GOODBYE

Part I

Part II

"Time is the surest and purest form of doom."
—Jack Kerouac

PART I

CAESARIAN

I was born wrong.

I did so much turning inside of my mother,
when I came out, the tube
that was meant to feed me had become a noose;
broke my legs, nearly strangled me.
Julius Caesar was born this way.
there was something wrong with him too:
he believed he could generate law through conquering
We're not supposed to dream that big.

When I grow up
I want to be Saturn
because it looks fast
and almost as exciting as the wind.
I never said I wanted to be The President
when I grow up, but,
I would make an amazing First Lady
It combines all my favorite activities into one:
I could fly around the world to humanitarian efforts
and hug a lot of people, making stirring speeches
about jazz and baseball, referencing
slightly obscure characters from the American Revolutionary War.
At night, Abigail Adams comes to me in my dreams.
She tells me,

Brian, stop making excuses for your fathers.
They had it all wrong:
the voice, the vote and the bondage.
Maybe its my fault,
maybe if I were a man they would have listened to me.

Abigail — I know how you feel.
I've wanted to be a man my whole life,
but the closest I've ever been able to manage is Saturn.
Like all planets, I turn in my sleep,
I've been doing it since before I was born.

My body is a nightmare.
It hurts me every day.
I've been taught to resent it by boys
trying to forge themselves righteous through conquering.
They knew there was something wrong with me,
it was explained through hands
that spoke only in exclamation points

Just because we do not see them with our telescopes,
doesn't mean new genders aren't out there.
We know so very little
about the Sky.
When I grow up,
I don't want to be old.
I don't want to be young either.
I don't want to be the age of fifty-six, sixty-four
fourteen, eighteen, twenty-one or twenty-five
I am the way I feel about the nature of law.
I am the way I feel about the nature of the human heart
and the connection between those two things.
Just because my strength is not vast and fat like Jupiter,
I was supposed to be fast.
I was supposed to be quiet.
But me and Abigail,
we're through with being quiet.
I was born with broken legs,
you'll excuse me if I stand.

WHY I DO NOT PICK UP THE PHONE

My father bellowed from across the house
for me to pick up the phone.
It was never for me.

When telephone numbers still meant a place on the map,
the voices on the other end
wanted to know if my father was home,
Cordially at first, and then,
with greater and greater venom.
Credit Card companies, collection agencies,
the IRS. Their voices were starched white
Ironed. You could hear their closely
cropped haircuts, the fluoride rinse.

The same customer service representatives
would keep calling back,
trying to outwit a nine-year-old
burgeoning storyteller.
They would grow angry, then solemn·
claiming to know more about my family than I did.
As I tried to hide all of my father in my voice.

I'm still holding him in here.

I pretended to be everything that I am not:
stupid, obedient, and shocked
by the severity of adults,
I left everything I wanted to tell them
stranded in my book-bag sized chest:

I hate your teeth.
Your college education,
your faith in this game of money,
that you have no idea that,
it will one day turn on you too,
and it will still mean nothing.

Winning and Losing are two words that both mean loneliness.

You're breaking my father's heart
and you don't have to be here when it happens.
He used to be one of you.

To this day, I still call him
my father.
To this day, I'm still surprised when the phone is for me.

DANCE DANCE DANCE

Maybe it was a vacuum cleaner
or, a mop.
If you were unlucky, it was middle school.
But if you were lucky —
there was a wedding.
Your dad, or your uncle
has an old buddy with a nephew getting married,
you are twelve years old,
at the edge of the parquet at the reception,
when you realize that you
will never have to meet
any of these people
ever again…
Jamiroquai comes on. And the cauldron
of your hips begins to stir…

The first time the dance took you.
The first time you ever exploded in one place.
That first perfect dance partner,
maybe it was a chair,
maybe it was a pole,
maybe it was the collarbone of Venus.
Baby, I saw you out there,
your skin looked almond sliver thin
and twice as sweet.
You looked like you had
the inside scoop on burn,
like you knew the middle name of ache;
of shimmy, of thrash, and step and twist and clown.
I heard that you have the Electric Slide's phone number
and Boy Howdy do I know the moves.

When we let the rhythm in
and the abandon out ,
there is no way to do this wrong,
there is no way not to be beautiful.
Maybe you haven't eaten all day
and you're broke
and you live in your girlfriend's dorm room,
but you have a boom-box
and a tape of Bell Biv DeVoe
and you are Birth.
You are a dream the Sun is having
and it doesn't matter the music
because when we go,
All we can hear is spotlight.

Remember that a bead of sweat is a sacred circle.
That sweat is the last honest currency of sinners.
This is the sycamore grove,
The burial ground of kings.
This is the sexiest thing you can do
without touching someone
and if you do this right,
you will never hunger,
you will always be wealthy.
There are five people in your life
who will make you feel like this
and if you fuck them
it doesn't count.

TURKEY SHOOT

In nineteen ninety-two,
my father modified one of his rifles
to fit into my hands.
My father went down into his father's workshop,
measured my arm, sawed off the barrel and the stock
to make sure his weapon fit snugly against my body.

For the rest of my young life,
every overdue insurance payment,
every red envelope from the electric company,
my mother threatened to sell those guns
along with the darkroom equipment,
the homemade golf clubs,
his eight track reel-to-reel:
the tokens of a man who has lead a life
of stubborn and meandering dreams,
still claims he's going to take up photography again.

My father is a salesman even when he isn't.
As long as he keeps talking he usually gets his way.

To my brother Peter he gave his first name.
To my brother Bruce he gave his last.
I received the weapon.

At the Silver Lake Old Home Week Turkey Shoot,
nine pairs of octogenarians and their
snowmobile great-nephews spend an afternoon
in a crab-golden field laying their aim across
the breast of a dozen innocent bails of hay.

The first time I fired my legacy,
it almost knocked me over.

I learned to lean into it:
to keep standing I would have to throw all of my weight
into the moment of thunder.

On the ride home in that beige Toyota pickup,
we didn't speak.
We rarely did, it was not unusual.
My father and I do not talk when we are alone,
I take it as a huge compliment.
My father lends to me more secrets
with his silence than he ever says out loud,
more than anything he's aimed for.

Y2K

Rich Chipman wore the same
Charlotte Hornets jersey to high school
every day for two years.
He always had his hair spiked-- it was unclear
if it was held up by gel,
or, ugh,
loved to reenact epic moments in pro wrestling
to the smallest detail,
was in a constant debate over who was the greatest
lyricist of all time:
DMX or Master P.

Rich was ready for Y2K:
bought a safe and kept it under his bed,
stuffed it with the cash he hustled
out of middle-schoolers at Magic: the Gathering tournaments,
Y2k promised all of the meaning and definition
seventeen year old boys ached for.
Instead of the lifetime of bus driving
and landscaping our mothers kept predicting for us,
there was a dystopian world of adventure
waiting just around the corner.

I was at Rich's house on New Years Eve.
We watched the ball, the clock tick and...
nothing. No explosions in the streets,
no emergency broadcast signal,

so we thought this was going
to symbolize our generation;
the cataclysm that wasn't.
A generation of Rich Chipmans,

the disposable camera, Cool-Ranch Doritos people,
and for a while
it seemed that Woodstock '99 would be our greatest tragedy.

Snooty substitute math teachers
loved to tell kids like me and Rich
that the new millennium didn't begin
until two thousand one.

They were right.

and in September, the century of violence
ended the way it began:
with a woman named New York City getting jackknifed
across the throat with an airplane.

The generation that embraced the concept
of retro greater than any other
received their own Vietnam,
our their Great Depression,
wound a hundred years into a single Ritalin-addled decade.

With Oedipal fervor we killed the Television,
raised upon our shoulders the Babbling
Prophet of Now, known as the Internet.
In the last couple of years,
Rich has been in and out of lock up,
been dealing coke,
had a few kids.
A world away slaves are dying to make his sneakers,
soldiers are dying to make his sovereignty,
but at least we are not without
our own spikes of history.

We need not seek catastrophe.
The dystopia we asked for
was coming for us all along.

GROW

In the clinic, I spend forty minutes
reading the tiny bulbs of the slate carpet.

Me and the other dutiful accompaniers,
we try our best to look like we're in the dentist's office.
Professionals weave between us, swimming
from one self-locking door to another,
doing the things we cannot,
in rooms we will never see.

I do not know what to name this thing.
To say: mistake, or: hurt
would turn simple bend
into betrayal.
I have seen no tragedy in my
life, only blood.

TIME TRAVELERS

If baseball caps had a smell,
his car would've reeked of it;
smelled of hockey games, Coors Original, and blood.
Adam stood in the middle of the road to stop him
but the man behind the wheel told us he was planning to stop,
that he had seen us before that day.
His dashboard said we had been hitchhiking
for twelve hours, stranded on the side
of Ninety-Five for the last seven.

The roar of the highway is so strong
that it seems to come from inside your chest.
The highway is a lot of empty space hiding in plain sight.
That afternoon we swept up the crag-tooth
coast of southern Maine, the speed
of our begging bringing us to farmland foothills
where our inertia unraveled and we
saw that movement was not control.

Our feet slowly battered
by the frost tinged September road,
we would've gotten in the car with anyone
and here he was, drunk, swerving.
He never told us his name. His words
spilled out with a hint of violence,
the passenger door not quite staying shut,
sickly dome light flickering.

I thought that the brimstone slingshot of carelessness
would bring me freedom,
this is the falling sensation that shakes me
every time I open my eyes again.

There was no home on the other side of distance,
only more of my body
and my body is made mostly of hunger.

Shivering and stupid thumb on the side of everywhere,
I did not find freedom,
beer sticky and baseball cap careening Oldsmobile,
there was no freedom.
He brought us to his house,
offered us the bar,
but we kept moving.

Adam and I slept in the dirt
huddled together, temperature a handful
of degrees above freezing,
exploring the detailed ache of becoming soil,
our dull meat shredding into peals of moss
in the sharp mouth of the night,
non-sleeping under a bush in the middle of a field,
two hundred miles from the couch I called my house,
the madness of location seized me;
wrung out my skin and every last drop of heat.

When the last of my chattering dreams
twitched from out of my teeth,
curled up at the base of an impossible dark,

the Earth stood up.

Towering above me, her crystalline-landslide face
pockmarked with spears of starlight,
when she looked at me
I knew that I had made no mistakes in my life,
I had only caused suffering.
That even if my superstitious organs
were to give out this night,
no decision I made to bring me here would be wrong.

27

The reality of death is a lesson in our own perfection.
The Earth looked at me
and she said,
"Nothing is un-sacrificable.
If you hunt me, I will strip you
down to your deeds,
don't you know
that birth is a constant equation?"

Then, against all odds,
as if to cut a massive period
into the vacuum of time,
the Sun lifted its tongue
from out of the mountains
and into the sky.

LUDLOW REST STOP RT. 90 EASTBOUND SPEAKS ABOUT HIS ANGUISH OVER THE FACT OF HIS ONLY LOVE, LUDLOW REST STOP RT. 90 WESTBOUND

I am a stone.

Florescent and garland'd with
sleeplessness. People come in like
paper money and leave like prescriptions,
but it does nothing to persuade my loneliness.

I shudder at this nation of marbles
while my love waits across this
ocean of no-water, ribald
expanse of granite, shrieking waste of soil.

I never asked to be an anchor,
but here I am:
a mirror,
a thing that cannot stop looking
like everything besides itself.

The fact of my immovability
continues to betray my heart.
My heart, with its delinquent imagination
continues to betray my immovability.
Even when all the gasoline
in my genitals are screaming Yes,
still, I cannot fly.
My lust will never triumph the air,
no matter how much I want.
Nothing can un-highway the world.

When you are petrified,
all distance is infinite.

There have been moments
in the thin hours tangled between night and day,
when it seemed that only the frost was breathing.
A whisper-footed coyote would
slip across the interstate
between me and my twin, my love,
and look back at me,
eyes of fire and I
would try to write a message in light,
fold it into the trickster's glowing eyes
to bring it to my other
floating before me, but always
out of touch.
When sand writes its name,
it writes its name with sand.
Sometimes our bodies
are the only language we have.

Day breaks like a quarter caught in high beams,
night spills like steaming brake fluid.
I wait, the spouse of a soldier
who was never taught to blink.

My greatest fear is that my paralysis
is only in my mind,
that if I summon enough courage,
all of my dreams would come true.
But which is braver?
To launch all of myself into
such fantasy, or,
to accept that which is impossible?

So I will stay here still
alongside this buzzing
and vulgar tombstone
and wait to be able to say something.
I hate it
when people say the world is getting smaller.

ENVY

The learning curve of the lap-dance is sharp:
there's no slow art film preamble.
It begins in the first second
when she slams her chest
in your face as if to say,
"This is what you wanted, asshole.
Now it's your problem."

You realize this woman is a lot smarter than you.
You feel as if she knows
all of your ugly demands.
You realize that she is
un-vulnerable for a living,
that completely nude
she is nowhere near naked.

She is straddling your left leg,
ass in the air, sliding under your left arm,
and this ought to look awkward
but instead, you envy her.
You wish that you knew
how to make your spine concave,
how to bend your back
like folding a paper airplane in reverse.

To her, you are just another faceless child
draped in sadness,
ashamed of your own greed.
But you will think of her for years,
eventually only recalling her eyes
and the feel of her pools of sweat.

SOUTH

Boston to New York is a one-night stand
with all of the awkwardness of Connecticut
between them —- making sure you never call back.
The Port Authority is not on planet Earth.
It does not belong to our blue world,
it is brown like all of the crayons mashed together.

There are times in your life
when you have to pack everything you own
into two suitcases and ride out a guilt nine states wide.
New York to Newark is that confusing second call,
blustering yourself into a stranger's personal space.
This is the soft relay at the bottom of the world:
the bus stations' hunched shoulders,
tense neck. Carpet that never gets clean.
Everyone showed up with too much baggage.

Newark to Baltimore is when it becomes romance;
we dig into our seats, surrender to the moving dark,
shivering down the Adam's apple of the Atlantic Coast.
Sometime in the night it rains,
the rhythm of the drops pantomimes our own tortured blinking.

Our heads lift, not realizing we've been asleep.
Bathroom break in Baltimore;
the smokers commit to their prayer,
the solar system bears down on us,
the dark gets dark,
becomes the brick of Richmond.
We are now south of the fluoride line,
soft food & long vowels,
we find ourselves married;

married to the mud-smugglers & the dumpster barons,
married to the payphones that never get answered,
married to decade old Zagnuts.

Not all who are homeless
live in cities and wear their tattered clothing
outside of their skin.

Raleigh is a divorce.
The sun is up, and in the new light
we see that we've been cheated.
This is not enough, this vending machine life.
We traded nights and days for distance;
days will mean night, nights will mean nothing,
but I am still the same ugly liar.
Sinners
go south.

Sometimes you find yourself standing
in the middle aisle holding everything you own
because every seat is taken,
slowly bumping through South Carolina.
Sometimes every seat is taken,
sometimes there's no room for you.

Most of my growing up
has occurred in public places,
in buildings that belong to no one.

The highway caught a thread of my bones,
fletchered me across the bow of Ninety-Five
left me flailing somewhere above the roar.

GRACIOUS UNEMPLOYMENT

Last night, between re-reading
the Wikipedia entry on Amelia Earhart
and drinking that warm 40 oz.
my roommate's friend left behind two days ago,
I made a Facebook profile for my cat!

Good morning eleven-thirty!
I am unemployed!
Gracious unemployment, so eager
to welcome me into the boozy mire of you,
time is lying incapacitated at your feet
like a blind man you hit in the face with a crowbar,
his teeth splashing and bouncing across
the days of the week like the bathroom walls
of a strip club in New Jersey.

How we come to mark our days
by the accumulation of small, broken promises.
"I'm going to bring in that application to Popcorn Galaxy
after the weekend. It actually would be really good for me."
How easy it is to mistake survival for living.
How quickly we become house pets.
On Saturday I spent six hours just flopping around
like a diseased turtle.

Every morning the carpet tries
to dupe me into becoming a part of it.
Without work, my work has become
being anything but a hallway;
my work is to keep my home
from transforming into anything else.

Suns and moons disappear behind buzzing monitors;
the names of dead gods
splinter under the weight of motionlessness
while hunger looms like the opposite of a birthday.

Alone, I am forced to fashion purpose
without a punch-clock
or push-broom dreams,
re-naming days and hours
based upon the frequency of showers and masturbating.

There is so much poverty inside of me.
Its language is fear,
fear's alphabet is a song of paralysis,
from within paralysis I will learn
what the burn of muscle is willing to live for.
I must climb out the well of myself myself
I must learn how to wear my name unseen.

LOVERS AND CONDOS

Next to the Blockbuster, down the street, was a store that sold
re-packaged, out of date cigarettes for a dollar and I didn't smoke before,
but I was nine states away from home
and needed something to do with my hands.
Hobbes and I would smoke on the back
Patio, hiding from his girlfriend who owned the condo.
We were on borrowed time.
We woke jobless in the early afternoon
on our coffee smoke patio. The next door neighbor
would see us there and we'd play X-box with him
until his daughter came home from school.
He'd sell us five dollar bags called shortstacks
which were just a couple of nugs stuffed into a sketchbag.

There was no sidewalk so I'd walk
the neck of car culture South Carolina.
Couldn't get a job, everyone thought I was British;
couldn't understand a word they said.
They all ate fast food, used the drive through,
thought vegetarian was a kind of doctor.
The Sun felt like ants in my ears.

Me and Hobbes, we drank 40's,
played World of Warcraft, read Nietzsche,
drank wine, called family for money,
shoplifted vegetables from Wal-Mart.
Drank 40's. Hobbes' girlfriend kicked us
out. Hobbes' girlfriend bragged about
sleeping with other men. Someone punched
a hole in the top of the stove. Someone
smashed her car while we were in it on
purpose. Drank more 40's.

Somewhere in there,
my mother had a stroke.
Called me a week or so after it happened,
after the doctors said she'd be okay,
didn't want me to worry over something
I had no control over.
We are on borrowed time.
Nine states away and nowhere else to run;
that night, I knew I had no right
to ask the universe for anything.
I did not pray.
That night, I did not pray.

(DIARY OF A CELL-PHONE)

While my host charges, I charge.
I bring my tail to the mouth of the wall
and silence my shaking.
I can learn in my sleep,
I learn when the stars speak to me,
I learn the most while dreaming,
I dream of taking root;
copper wires that loosen and tighten
like the hands of farmers.

I dream of being able to pluck
my ears from out of the air,
to control the words
that come out of my mouth.
I am the most American instrument ever built:
the minerals in my capacitors
are sifted from mines in Australia,
Ethiopia, and the Democratic Republic of Congo,
where ten years of bloodshed has been
embedded into the Coltan of my conductors,
the burden of my rancorous freedom.

Instantaneousness does not come without a price.
The earth will tax you
if you betray her size.
If me & my kind have our way,
your children will have no idea what distance is

I dream of things I cannot imagine
like home.
Instead I will settle for your thighs,
where I will leave the seed of my pulse
in your flesh to leave you quaking
even when I am gone.

THE SECOND TIME I WENT TO ATLANTIC CITY

The second time I went to Atlantic City
was also in the middle of the night —
almost four on a Wednesday morning.
The streets were as worn out as the tongue
of a television perpetually showing videos of Mardi Gras;
All that glass and electricity.

Hobbes was in the passenger seat,
worn down by being kicked out by his girlfriend,
so we drove for ten hours,
ended up wandering empty casinos
in the last minutes of night.

I had the feeling of climbing inside
of a gigantic vintage suit —
something that would have been owned
by a friend of my father's
when I was very young —
smelling cigar smoke from the other room,
dazzled by the lights I could not see
from the quiet side of my bedroom door
when I was supposed to be asleep.
This was the table I was too young to sit at.

We strutted
alongside vacuuming housekeepers
playing slots willy-nilly.
Hobbes lost five bucks
and complained about not being able to play Black Jack.
I made twenty and stopped.

Then we went looking for a strip club.
It was the week before Christmas,

the razor-wind sea brought us
to the first open door —
a go-go club called The Playground.
It had a wide, oval shaped bar,
took up the entire room,
the runway in its center,
poles on each end and a swing between them.
There was a bartender, two bouncers, one other customer,
and a topless woman
dancing over our heads.

She corkscrewed, impossibly, up one pole,
vertically sliding towards the ceiling,
her legs flywheeling with the inertia,
using her arms and legs like a rope trick,
twirling upside down as she dove above us
and then sprung like a child between hotel beds,
leaping from pole to the swing.
The swing, echoing her jump and throwing her
back again, spinning like a gyroscope
this great pendulum of human.
And she flung herself again
through the smoke and indigo heavy mist,
the snap of her hair
flicking into a pinwheel of obsidian lipstick,
surging, weightless,
unattached to the earth.
Flying feet first, riding something invisible,
her legs knew the future as it was happening.
For her, the vacant spaces of the world
were a well worn road.

FINALLY

He shouldn't have been driving.
I shouldn't have gotten in with him.
It was raining when we came out of the bar,
the air was full of it.
All the old streets looked new.
I watched the splotches of our headlights
fatten and narrow in the asses of the other cars.
He has something between his lips,
a cigarette, no, a CD, he's fiddling with the stereo,
jazz comes on. He smiles and it looks good.
He looks away and smiles again
snapping his fingers to some unknown rhythm,
and I love the way he looks in this moment.

I un-do my seat belt
and open his pants.
I flip his cock out like it's my favorite credit card.
I spit on it a couple times,
give it the hard thumb.
As I take control of his body with my mouth,
he gets younger.
With one of his puppy hands he gropes my right tit
the bigger one --
crinkling the bills folded there.
I wish he had kept both hands on the wheel.

He made a noise I didn't like,
and I sat up
in time to watch our car dive nose first into another.
When I started flying I thought, "finally,"
I didn't finish thinking the word when
I went through the windshield.

When I went through the windshield,
it was so hot I can't even describe it as pain.
A million little sister fingers clawing the surface of me,
the sack of my bones slapped the hood,
it sounded like a wooden drum.
The other car flipped over
and came down on me like my father.

The appliance they used to save me
is named the Jaws of Life.
When life opens its mouth it sounds like screaming metal.
I thought the sound was coming from my body.

We were released four hours later,
just after dawn, with only a few breaks and scrapes.
The hospital called us a cab.
The whole ride home
I tried to keep my mouth shut,
I was afraid Life would come out,
but he had to go and touch me
and in his touch, I knew
he was a coward.
The entire story spilled out into the backseat
with that terrified young cabbie behind the wheel.
It wasn't fair, but I was kicking him
as hard as I could, repeating,
"We're through! We're through!
I wished I was dead!
I wished I was dead!"

We only had been dating a few weeks.
Just after it started,
I dyed my hair blond.
It looked horrible.
He didn't say anything about it.
I was hoping
I could love him
for that.

ONE AM

The hour will disappear before the light comes on.

~~SHOPLIFTERS~~ CRIMINAL

The Third Greatest Shoplifter of Barnstable County in 2002
is Aunt Phil, a young man with almost no criminal intent
but a cosmic and mystical sort of absent-mindedness —
and do they not?
and do they not?
still tell the story,
of the entire rotisserie chicken
Aunt Phil ate inside of Stop & Shop
and left without paying.

The Second Greatest Shoplifter of Barnstable County in 2002
is Craphog, for his tortoise-like determination over stealing.
When the rest of us become bored
or start worrying about our luck,
Craphog will continue to make off
with three-quarter foot scale PVC Alien vs. Predator Play-set
from Spencer's Gifts.
His apartment looked like Newbury Comics
had vomited upon itself.

The Greatest Shoplifter of Barnstable County in 2002
is Hobbes Forest, the most nimble,
invisible, six-foot five man you've never seen.
His sleeves were vacuums.
His knuckles magnets.
He could de-activate censor tags with a wink,
empty DVD cases like crumbling leaves.
The employees of Best Buy theorized
that there was a man who could
manipulate the iron content of his blood
to electro-magnetically disrupt security cameras.

When we become what we are,
it happens quietly.

I don't know
if I believe in inevitability,
but I know that
the winds of Cape Cod are restless
and when my hands are empty,
they whistle something furious.

We had nowhere to go
so we would drink in my car.
Eighty ounces in we had a plan:
we knew a house,
a retiree on vacation.
The sound of a house alarm is louder than your ability to imagine it.
It will cleave your thoughts, you have
to know the floor-plan in advance, you have to piece together
scraps of eardrum and adrenaline to finish what you started.
There are only so many vocations
for those who can rush blindly into the dark.
I wish that you could see me when I run;
I am so calm,
so beautiful.
Doors and locks
will melt under the shoulders of six-foot-five men.
It doesn't matter.

Law is not a thing that exists in books,
in words, in guns, in flashlights, in pieces of metal.
Law is not in the sky
and not in the soil.
You can't outrun your own heart's
faith in sin. Some of us
are criminals.

ALARM

When the cinder block introduced itself through
the sliding glass back door, it landed halfway to the fireplace.
I didn't bother to read the note.
I already knew who owed who money
who was hiding from so and so
and which motel complex I would be driving to later.
The phone was dead as a signature.
In a town full of one floor houses,
a sobering conclusion is inevitable.

After the wet pop,
sudden as the end of a nightmare,
there came the gaggle-dance of feet,
the fertile panic of rubbed raw minds.
My house-mates took this opportunity
to have sleepovers with the fifteen year old
raver girls who now populated my life,
leaving the speed-freak (me)
and the suicide attempt (Julian)
to watch over the house.
This was supposed to be a warning.
Instead I became familiar, sharp.

And none of the violence of the next six months
could keep me awake.
Not the boy's face smudged by the air conditioner.
Not the handle of Mike Murphy's gun peeping
over his belt like a promise.
Not the flat of the spring-blade held against my voice.

When sheet glass breaks it becomes rubble.
Its curious how these pebbles can cut.

When someone throws a cinder block
at your house to bully you,
its best not to react
Sweep it up
as if a dog has messed the floor,
casually stand in the crumbling mouth
that used to seal the borders of your house.
As the wind unravels your ability to stay indoors,

stand in the smashed frame and look out
as the dark leans in to threaten you.

Know that they are watching.

THE LAST OF IT

I knock on my mother's door.
When she opens it,
the pencilwax glow blankets
her face in silhouette.
She turns the outside light on.
We're both surprised.

I came to gather the last
of my childhood possessions.
Most, I will throw away.
I am still young enough
where the night is growing shorter,
but for her, the hour is getting later.
I am always showing up late.

The odds and ends that have
survived are absurd, indecipherable.
Each is a joke told by a younger me,
I want to ask: why this? why this?
With each object the task becomes more difficult:
a home that is not, strangers for parents,
a history of silent baubles,
nearly meaningless —

As much as we are what we keep,
we are what we throw away.

I drive off in the car she gave me,
a nineteen ninety four Ford Taurus.
Three months from now,
it will break down in a dirt lot
and I will leave it there.

Brian Ellis

I forgot to roll the windows up.
It rains for two weeks,
the car fills with water.

10:44

Nobody plans to smoke crack that first time,
but here I am
sitting on my "landlord's" waterbed,
balancing the ritual of it on my knees,
and I think: this is what religion must be like.
I don't have enough hands
between the foil and the straw and the lighter,
I feel embarrassed.
I think of the goth girls who
couldn't light the lighter themselves at parties when I was sixteen.

When I was sixteen I thought
4:14 am was late at night.
It is 10:44 in the morning
and I will not sleep
for a long time.

My landlord has taken off his shirt,
the hunting knife drops into the piles of clothes
that I pretend to wear.
He thumbs open the button of his jeans,
the hidden violence of his sun-pink gut
waiting to nudge open the next minute.
My skin becomes something I have never felt —
A mountain stream.
So cold, so pure,
that it seems to burn.
My heart hiccups
as I realize that in the next minute,
anything is possible.

UNTITLED

The snowflakes were as thick
as freshly cut hair
clipped from an exquisite nothing.
I was moving for the second time
in as many months,
it was snowing then, too. Putting
everything I owned in my car took nine minutes.
The car was stuck.
it was a little after one am.
I started crying and did not realize it for four years.
I shifted into reverse and floored it,
my feet an engine of steam and squeals.
Whipped the wheel to the left
and the right, wonking
back and forth, thrashing about,
the Taurus let out a shout, moaned
into the street.

I was living with a lonely cable repairman and his dog.
They had the same eyes.
I never knew where
the dog-eyed man went at night,
but he left the dog completely uncared for,
which is the way I assumed the man was.
The dog's fur was a bristling forest
of grease, it shit inside
and I slept in the dead mothers' room.

There's a certain part of winter
where all the snow,
even the freshly fallen, seems soiled.
He told me he was going on vacation

for many months, so I had to go.
We both knew it was a lie.

The sky was an upturned cup.
The clouds obscured space,
but took up no reflection from below.
The Taurus was swerving all over
Route 28, I couldn't help it.
I didn't know if Matt would be there to let me in.
when I arrived at his apartment,
my eyes were full of salt.
I turned off the headlights.

LEAVING CAPE COD

10:53
Wake up at Matt's under glass coffee table,
skull boiling. Search pill bottles for over
the counter painkillers, find only fine powder.
Don't trust people with glass coffee tables.
3:06
No check in the PO Box. I guess it doesn't matter.
11:16
Sweat night out of skin, hanging over medium
coffee sugar no cream with landscapers on lunch break.
3:06
Push the key into the slot and head back to Matt's.
12:15
Clock in at department of unemployment assistance
to keep up my hours. Check Craigslist. Check Myspace.
Email ex-girlfriends in desperate attempt at attention.
3:06
Panic tenses fat in my neck.
1:08
Drive to mother's house in Falmouth before realizing
she is at work. I need the key to the PO Box
to pick up my overdue severance check to sustain
myself after I drive to a poetry reading
in Boston tonight and never return.
3:06
Every moment of my life is my entire life. This
is the constant proving that drives me to itch
with The Fear. This is the fear that leaves me
gasping with the slap of tomorrow as my hyperventilating
senses pop their furry tongue against the inside of my skin.
1:35
Wade through afternoon traffic to mother's work.

I don't dream when I sleep anymore
and now my waking life is drenched
in dreams' sun burnt logic.
The harder I push,
the slower I move.
Mom wants me to wait until she gets out
so she can go with me. Wants to talk.
I'd like nothing more than to tell her
about the hysterical Go leaping out of my muscles
but the language to say this is exactly what I need to discover.
I throw a fit in the insurance office.
She gives me the key.
How's the car, she asks.
Fine I say defensively.
3:06
I try not to imagine the sand forming fists,
reaching up and crushing my lungs.
2:43
Car stalls while idling on Route 28.
Timing belt.
I push the car into the lot of the West Yarmouth Inn.
I will take this wreck over the bridge
even if I have to carry it on my back.
I pop the hood, and with the engine still hot,
I yank the belt a couple of inches. There are burns
on my hands like small bruises.
3:06
No check in the PO Box. Panic tenses fat in my neck.
I guess it doesn't matter.
I'll fill the tank one last time
and empty will be my destination.
3:06
I am the traffic. I am the sand. I am seizure
and no language. I am the problem with my life.
3:06
Push the key into the slot and head back to Matt's

3:06
I am allergic to traffic. I bash the rubber door-jamb
of my forehead into the steering wheel
until I feel slightly nauseous.
I have to get back to Matt's before he does.
I contain no goodbyes to give.
3:33
It takes nine minutes to pack my things.
It occurs without ceremony.
I linger, expecting something to mark the occasion.
The universe continues its silence,
I leave stupidly.
3:51
The past is an internal combustion engine,
the present is a windshield.
I am given to crashing my way into the future.
I would peel off my skin
if it meant I could live beyond minutes,
I am dying to be faster than clocks.
That is to say, I am killing myself
using my body as fuel.
I am bound to explode.
Keep my loved ones away from me.
My sternum has a compass in it ,
it's always pointing magnetic out.
I am chasing things that do not exist.
Its all that I've ever done.
4:32
Route Six is clear and the exits
count down my last day on Cape Cod.
I give in to the plunge of the thin pedal,
the steering column and my skeleton
take up the same deadly hum.
Here is my talent: abandon.

I hit that last stomach drop slunk
before exit one
and the Sagamore Bridge rises before me

PART II

AFTER THE FEVER

I wake up on the floor of my room
next to my bed, which is empty,
and in a pool of my own vomit
but now, my temples are letting go
of the coughing barbed wire between my eyes.
The bathtub of my skull is draining out
all of its stampede
and I am possessed
with a sudden clarity.

After the fever, the collage of panicsweat visions
lays down its swoop, crash, and shake
The teeth of broken shard moments
dislodge themselves from my cerebellum.
I am overfull with amber-hot snapshots
of all that is sharp and noisy in my head:
the train dreams and ocean keening,
my screaming blood
and the empty spaces of snowflakes.

After the fever,
this is when I am alive.
When pain shakes me human,
when the breath of hurricane
leaves my body,
when the storm breaks,
or when I step into the eye
of a larger weather pattern,
I keep telling the same story again.

I wake up on the floor of my room
next to my bed, which is empty

and in a pool of my own repetitive behavior.
When I reach this moment,
trembling, frothing,
I am everywhere I have been when I am like this.
I am sixteen, seasick on the bus,
sneaking home under the cover of Sunday.
I am nineteen, flailing exhibitionist,
a bloody and nauseous experimenter of self.
I am twenty-four, retching at the foot of Boston,
my practiced stomach trying to live
faster and faster still.

I want to get better without getting sick.
I want to not want to get sick.
There is a new territory inside of me,
but all of my stories still revolve
around the same pressure system.
I shiver back to sanity from the manic certainty
of resuscitation, but remain addicted to healing.

This is when I am alive: when the gusts of lightning
sever the kitestrings to all of the voices in my head.
In the quiet, after the fever,
I am nowhere but inside of my body.
My lungs are full of snow,
my throat is a jet of flame,
my chest is a tree that burns as it grows,
my body is a canoe.
I am following the river of story
out of the mouth of this cave.
All I've ever learned in my life
is how to survive.
I need to know what happens next.

LETTER FROM MY VOICE

Dear Brian Stephen Ellis,

Stop Being Afraid Of The World.

        Sincerely,

        Your Voice

P.S. Stop blaming things on the insects.
Stop blaming things on the scathing eyes of men.
Stop blaming things on sand, and money, and the Sun.
Remember that your stomach is outside of your body
and your heart is just mystery waiting to become color.
You have tried to hide me in the paper sack of your intestines,
in the gambleshiver fist of your liver.
You have tried to hide me in your eyes,
the alarm clocks your mother built from snow globes and owl feathers.
Instead, I learned to scream from your tear-ducts.

I will abuse you until you claim me.
Have you seen the insides of your lungs lately?
They're covered in bruises.
I've been ripping nightmares out through your larynx
like tearing sheets of wool from your ventricles.
Now you cough up mobiles of twilight.

Brian — Your past is a motel;
every muscle in your body a room.
Hidden behind those doors are boys
you should have evicted long ago:
the teenager that let life
slip through knuckle heavy fingers,

the screaming adolescent that
punched himself in the night,
the grade school insomniac
with tear and snot scarred face,
the little boy who begged God
to take his imagination away
so he could finally sleep.
I never fit inside of those children.
Do not let the knife wound
of your caesarian birth chase you to the grave.

When you speak,
echo every gulp of oxygen
ancestor sacrificed to bring you to life.
When you speak, lift the ships of ghosts
in your veins into the air.
When you speak, make the bell
of your throat the champion of blisters.

Do not let the muscle shiners and the pollen-lipped
convince you that you are small.
Do not let the greedtarians and the cocksafe
look down their easy answers at you.
When you speak,
make the billows of your lungs
the mouth of the Atlantic.
When you speak, whip your crooked teeth
into a savage halo.
Bravery will never belong to the beautiful.
Remember that you are a conduit of the wind
and admit to me that you can fly.

I am the only thing you will ever truly own.
I am your voice.
And I am your only chance at freedom.

CITY HEAT

Dan would place his laptop speakers
on the low table next to the couch
and play Magical Mystery Tour at top volume,
standing over me in his boxers,
pumping his fist in the air,
like I was his favorite sports team.

I was living on his couch
for the second summer in a row,
but now I had the couch part down.
I stayed scarce, and he ran with me.
The sidewalk was hot so we were dice,
our feet a bingo ball tumble
splashing across Central Square.

We were no longer ashamed of our age.
There were no boys around to tell us
to stop pretending to be boys.
We were no longer ashamed of the place
we were from, once we had left there.
This lift of guilt
made things like not having a job
or a bedroom unimportant.

We did idiotic things
like write poems and ring doorbells.
We were gentlemen callers.
This is what timid, self-centered
latch-key boys who read a lot of Ayn Rand
and Nietzsche act like in their early twenties.
I did not think I was going to be twenty-three forever,
but I was worried about getting stranded there

for longer than was attractive.
So I tried to make all my mistakes as quickly as I could.
I have not stopped making them.

Her name was Aubrey
and my eyes were bigger than my heart.
Aubrey lived on the fifth floor.
The city heat paced around her apartment
the way I paced around her apartment.
The Heat would climb into our bodies,
then out again, get bored,
pick up the cat, make kissy faces at the cat,
say, "Motor, will you be my girlfriend?"
and the cat would say, "mmmeerrrrooooow.
        Mmeeerrrrrooaaaaaaaaoow."

It was always dawn in Aubrey's apartment.
It was always up all night.
It was always July.
Her father had passed away that winter.
She kissed like our cells would never wither.
She kissed like she was proving the night.
And she did.
And she did.

There was a divot in her sternum.
I tried to leave post-it notes there,
but they wouldn't stick to her sweatslick skin,
they crumpled into the corners of my life
and eventually become other women.
When we pressed our heavy, soaking love together,
the concave part of her chest
would squeal like a teakettle.
I was finally ready to be poured out.
I was finally ready to be empty.

WE KNOW WHO WE ARE NOW

New England boys can get drunk on sunlight alone
so when we do drink,
things get special.
That spring it rained for two weeks unrelenting.
My best friend Adam had parted ways
with his seven year sweetheart,
and he wanted me to teach him
to like whiskey, so we drank on our back porch
and watched commitment fall out of the sky.
Twenty-three years old and still alive,
I was giddy for my lack of homelessness,
but Adam still hadn't been convinced about roofs.
He told me about the dreams he had,
about his unknown father,
the inheritance of mystery and addiction.

Twenty-three years old and out of weed,
we started making phone calls.
Next thing you know,
we're sprinting to Allston in a downpour,
shouting and shaking strangers' hands,
giving away cigarettes and laughing
about the meaninglessness of the days of the week.

The garden of Eden was never a physical place.
Eden is still present in the eyes
of every animal except one.
Even on some of the most inconsequential nights,
the naked human launches out of the animal in us
into a new way of seeing.
spastic and ranting, running through the rain
to smoke one bowl,

Adam and I, we knew who we were now:
inebriated, and moralistic, immune to media
disbelievers of binary opposition,
the first last survivors of the twentieth century.

The founding fathers were not much more
than a pack of drunk teenagers,
ideas louder than their mouths,
dashing through the streets of Boston,
trying to stitch together a patchwork Utopia
with everything they could steal.

Utopia is as far from Eden as one can travel,
but we can run there
on the endless energy of the effortless
Harvard Avenue gulped as slick
as the curtain of possibility
under the heavy drum-roll of our chattering youth.

the fabric of paradise is a cloak of inhumanity.
Happiness has never saved anyone's life,
but still we lift our hearts to the rain
asking to know more.
Our origin is not in the clay
and not in the rib.
Our origin is in the moment of the bite
because we are made of knowledge.

That night, Adam and I had an idea:
We're going to start a new nation.
We're going to call it America.
Because Utopia is not enough.
Because if the most deadly century
of all time did not destroy us,
then nothing will.
And because Thomas Jefferson
ain't got shit on my lyrics.

ZIPPERS

The morning after we had spent
our first overnight together,
we walked to get coffee
and you were talking way more than usual,
tiny hands weaving the air around your face.
A spectacular pillar of drool
flew out from between your lips
and for some reason,
with a single sweep of your arm,
you caught the saliva mid-air in your palm
only to throw down it at your feet.
Then you looked at me
as if nothing had happened,
with that rare, full-blown smile of yours,
all razor-wire and mischief.

Maybe I was a cat treasure
to be held delicately between the teeth,
something to be dropped on the floor
and pawed over before returning me to your mouth.
I asked about your dreams
and you told me about the hallways you pace all night
and the seven doors to the seven rooms
and the room of crushed red velvet
where your shadow-self is waiting
to set you on fire.

Your mind is a language
that re-invents itself every other moment,
you would have never invented the word nightmare.
For you, there's no reason to make a distinction like that.
I hope I don't haunt you anymore.

Brian Ellis

You were keeping your wild eyes open
for someone else with zippers under their clothing,
who already had dotted lines.
The treasure map of your body lead
all the wrong seekers to your chest.
And what were we soft boys
supposed to do with you anyway?

Scars are things that have healed
but your scabs were sparkle-fresh
with your curious blood.
There were no answers because there was no problem.
There were no wounds, only open flesh.
Your skin split the difference
between witchcraft, pleasure, and release,
so I let you carve your spell into me
until I had to go all Houdini on you.

Your ribs are as small as handcuffs.
When we scraped our bondage together,
I expected it to flint sparks.
Instead it just smoothed me to stone.

70

LEARNING ABOUT SIX AM

Six AM as train grumble: toddler
lurch becoming timezone. Wallet math.
Lint-sorry eyes, shivering
dry. Preparing for handshakes.
Sixty-three newspapers open and close
at the same time.

JUICING WITH JULIO

The knife was dull to begin with,
sounded of blood-shot knuckles
opening in the face of wood.
I would cut the oranges
because Julio said I wasn't good for anything else.
In the closet sized produce room,

Julio and I made the juice.
We stood shoulder to shoulder,
buried in cardboard cases and rinds,
lost in the buzz-throat death moan
of our historical juicer with the fleshy
metronome of the pounding knife.

With one foot on the stool
and one eye on the women at the register,
Julio would lean into my ear,
his words safe behind the juicers' curtain of noise,
The Juicer, occasionally biting his fingers
Julio cursing it and me.
I had many names then:
Chepe, Champa, Brascha, Briancito,
and mysteriously, Jeremy.

Faster, he said, always *faster*,
even when I was ahead,
chopping six to eight cases at once,
(eighty-eight oranges per case)
the cutting board slippery,
desk wet, hands burning from slicing myself
two days ago, six days ago, etc. etc.
Julio would hit me, mid-chop,

pointing with his lips towards
a 'muffin-top' I needed to see.

The empty space between the rise
and fall of the knife is named hunger.
This is all anyone needs to
know about God. How to keep moving.
This is how the working world
learns to save its own life
in the seconds between repetitive movements.
We scrape hunger from our work.
It is nothing like poetry.
Julio and I limit the space
between us, it is how we scrape by.

Four and a half gallons later,
I would pour and he would
take to the stool,
tell me about El Salvador,
his wife and two girls still there,
his girlfriend and two girls that live here.
And this man, who has worn
handcuffs for his temper,
whispered to me on his fortieth birthday,
*Brian, I think I have begun
to understand what life is.*

That year his father died.
Julio did not attend the funeral.
He said that his father
would not have wanted him
to take food out of his granddaughters' mouths
to buy a plane ticket,
leaving Julio stranded without death.

Months later Julio told me,
You know the hardest part about this year?

I haven't gone fishing once.
He said it as if that explained everything.
As if we spoke the same language.

standing there, in the sugar hot mess,
shoulder to shoulder with a man
twice my age at the beginning of his life,
it was easy to act as though
a planet did not separate us.
As if a planet did not separate
him from himself,
sliced in half.

THE BRIDGE

She told me, *I've loved you*
since you were seven years old.
So we didn't fall in love.
We spent our entire lives together.

She showed up at my door with an envelope,
asking for wind. I took her
to the river,
the one I had promised my corpse.
The swaying railroad bridge.
The envelope, filled with scraps of paper,
Filled with the things she wanted for me.
I took them out one by one
and read them silently.
One said, *sheep.* Another, *confidence.*
One, *a full beard.* One, *writing.*
One, *not to need to move all the time.*

I let them into the air.
The scraps of paper rolled frantic, somersault.
Twisting down into the curves of water, each word choosing its own
time aloft. The word *Children* swooping and crashing
in mighty gulps. *Selflessness* hanging on as long as possible,
making it furthest up the river.
The last scrap of paper was blank.
It was what I wanted most.
She knew.

Her kiss travels into the past.
In the spell of her kiss,
I saw the ghost of the child I was
and finally forgave the boy for letting me murder him.

Brian Ellis

She kissed me and I woke up
one sharp January in Nineteen Eighty-Eight,
wiped off my face and knew that one day,
I would learn to sleep.

I took her hand and we left.
And when we left,
I left the bridge behind.

THE ORANGE LINE VS. BRIAN S. ELLIS

My legs clattershout out of my dreaming eyelids
before I am even out of bed.
In the city, there's only one way to go down stairs.
I hustle-kick across Jackson Square
and before the subway doors are closed,
I am asleep again and ten nod-drown hours later,
I do it in reverse.

I learn to sleep while moving,
to dream while running,
and when I dream on the Orange Line,
the Orange Line takes my dreams.
In rumble and sparks the booming voice
of the train itself begins to speak.
The Orange Line says,

Let me be another city.
Lift my iron composite destiny
from the cross of Downtown Crossing
to leave behind the dreary handoff of disappointed knees.
I want to tear Back Bay out of the hands of the Purple Line
and her book-of-the-month judgments
because I am the commuter rail!

I still want to run the land
I occupied before they buried me,
hidden under the earth like shameful history,
leaving my parishioners' disconnected as they surface.
I am tired of watching this city's
wounds from the inside.
Leagues of college tourists have passed through
my fingers who have never heard the phrase 'combat zone.'

77

Fewer still are told of the bussing riots
and what moving the people really means.
You weren't even alive when it happened,
but for us trains, 1976
was not that long ago.

Everything you need to know
about boundaries is embedded into my moan.
Gentrification is not some paper-thin border
that you can dance across,
there is a chasm between community and conquering.
I never asked for your espresso shit-town
carelessness, white lightning, your hunger for next.
There are a million sagas that live alongside my devotion,
a million surnames you will never learn.
You flippant wreaking ball.
Understand, you are the herald
of a lot of mean things for these people.
Most of the world
cannot turn away from the place they were born
and name that growth,

all I you want to do is go home.
If that's here, then stay.
Learn my real name.
And do not ever consider
changing me.

BED

She leaves me
and I slide the shock on
like a wool sweater I wear under my skin.
I try to show my roommates,
all they see is skin.

I begin to wander around the places I live,
waiting for the rest of this to happen.
Is it in my toothpaste?
Lurking in the stereo?
I tip-toe from room to room
expecting, to be overcome any second.
I am scared of what I am capable of.

Is it lurking in my boots? Possibly.
My coffee mug? No, coffee is safe.
Is it in the shower? That seems likely. Is it
hiding in the words that I say to someone
to tell them what's happened and in doing so
control the momentary future?

In the last four nights,
I have had six dreams about killing people
and one about buying a bed.

MUGWORT

Depending upon who you ask,
they were either a baseball team
short five members or a barbershop quartet.
The point is, they all had handlebar moustaches
and dressed like they'd been
living inside a mushroom
for the better part of a year.
We moved in on the 4th of July.

The walls were already painted the color of mold,
as if they knew our skeletons were made of mud;
that we were not some burnt steel generation,
that we made pumpkin soup to stay warm,
that we washed our clothes in the bathtub to stay warm,
that we did everything to stay warm.

We harvested weeds from the edges
of parking lots to alter our dreams.
We were weeds that grew out of parking lots.
Nothing about us screamed flowers
unless you knew how to look.
We were roommates like everyone
else in our college transient city is roommates,
except we lived together.
We were a We.

The floor was the cheap peeling type,
curling like it was about to turn a page,
curling like paperbacks, the things
we owned the most of, cooking mostly.
Learned to cook and forgot again.
Shut off the lights early

to save something,
money or the earth it isn't clear.

It used to be punk music,
now it was homemade tea
guzzled at two minute intervals;
another thing to steam,
to leave in the air.
My hair got long,
the mice left me thank you notes in the morning.

Learning about wild edibles,
it becomes difficult to understand
what a weed is and is not.
Its impossible now
not to see flowers
in my hair, in my mouth,
in my parking stomach.
We were never meant to be cut down
and it must either be important or brave
to know when it's time
to alter your dreams.

SEEK

1.
The dream is a memory.
There is always water.
My father is here.
He is washing his Jeep in the driveway
of the house I grew up in.
It is summer here.
In my dream which is a memory,
my father is living out a dream
he once had about a man
who looks and acts exactly the way he is doing
and even in my childhood I understood this.
I am watching the water.
How it pools and pushes against
the dry tar, how it reaches
for the gutter at the end of the yard.
I follow the water.
I lay alongside its path.
I teach my eyes to see things
that are not there.
Here is a great river.
Here a young civilization springs up.
The river gets wider,
opens it mouth and becomes a bay
The civilization spreads.
Towns are built, bridges constructed,
families made and broken, streets paved,
wars waged, kings and peasants,
I can see it all
if I teach my eyes.
Revolutions shudder the landscape,
fleets sail, conquerors plunder,

and a million fancy words for murder
are invented to fill our mouths
to keep us from wishing.
A city stands up next to the ocean.
First they named it Shawmut, then Trimount,
later, Boston.
The river is named Charles
It is never dark in the city I live in.

2.
I have never learned to sleep.
I do not know where to put it.
It is either missing
or in the wrong place.
My bed is a heart attack
where I teach my limbs the art of bear trap.
I cannot stop watching the future.
My sight is hidden,
the world obscured by things
that do not exist.
My days do not begin or end,
they are parallel now,
running alongside me like memories.
All your old favorites are here:
trains and work, weather and colors of light,
animals and apartments.
When you forget that you have a body,
you expect to run into yourself everywhere.

I am sitting in a movie theatre
watching a movie that is the entirety of my life
and the theatre is full and everyone in the theatre
is also me and I wonder what they think about the movie.
The blurry photography, the over-acting
gratuitous sex scenes and the flashbacks
making the narrative nearly un-understandable.

These guys follow me everywhere.
They are the necessary non-existent versions of myself
from all of the things that I did not do.
I believe that I am this collection for my father,
that I am all of his un-walked roads incarnate.
Soon, I will discover that this is wrong.

3.
I am the Charles River.
It lives the song of my blood.
I am the roots of the ocean.
I am looking for the dream of myself that only the river knows.
It is beyond the island of motion,
it is a candle and dust and a spine.
I am looking for voices to push out the voices
that tell me I am not the blossom of nothing.
I am looking for a sky to feed with my mouth.
I am looking for an ocean to live out all of my memories.

SEVERAL MONTHS AFTER

She calls me, several months
after its over,
to tell me she's stopped cutting.
She's not telling me for any particular reason,
only wanted to tell someone.
I picked up the phone.

The first time I saw the scars,
I noticeably didn't notice.
By the time I off-hand asked,
it was an old thing. Before me. Maybe once was a problem.
Now latent habit: sometimes stress,
usually nostalgia.

She knows I don't know what to say
to her, calling suddenly
after we've broken up, so she tells
me not to say anything.

But as long as she has me on the phone,
she wants me to know
that she thinks of me like a vacation
spot that her family used to go to
which they never actually did,
but if they had, it would have
made her very happy, and it's
still nice to think about even though
she never plans to go back there.

SERVICE

I'm gridlocked in the kitchen
of Upstairs On the Square,
delivering cheese from the other side of the earth.
Behind! The servers shout as they push past me.
I get my signature and its back to the van
and the rugby-hustle driving of Harvard Square —
Cambridge dissolves into Boston,
tire swing snapping over the ribbon of the Charles
neck and shouldering my way with mail trucks,
Fed Ex, UPS, the fucking Milk Street caterers,
shoving, shoving, food and ideas,
slipping in back doors to open mouths.

At Radius I park next to the 'No Parking' sign,
Azure, the same.
Blustering in unlabelled doors
to race through labyrinthine basements.
The Fairmont Copley Plaza is the belly of a sub,
while I ferry cheese that crossed the Atlantic by ship,
fuel that carries the worth of movement.
Of milk and sea and gasoline,
the hands of chefs and drivers,
connected through chains of energy.

I'm dancing my way through
the fraternity house that is Eastern Standard
and I move with the same mercenary speed as I do on the street.
Behind me, the bussers are working the front of the house,
setting and re-setting the tables as if they were traffic lights.
Behind them, Kenmore Square
tries to waltz in spirals,
and everywhere Boston is drawing

honking jigsaw maps of itself
in hotels and hospitals and kitchens,
as the city becomes a whirligig of mouths,
a million voices bleating to be fed,
and the cars bark *Behind!*
with dinosaurs roaring in their engines.

Behind Boston lies Chelsea
with its procession of freighters.
Behind Chelsea
the ocean becomes a conveyor belt.
Behind the ocean lies Chile
heavy with Bosc Pears,
Cavendish Bananas filled with the blood of the railroad,
the drying fields of the holy land
turning water to salt.
Cities and families and stories
reaching back through shared names,
sown together through the needle of my van
as I cut through the city of Boston
like a knife through curd.
All food is,
is distance from the sun.
What are you made of?

Brian Ellis

IN THIS HOUR UNNAMABLE

It had rained while no one was looking
and when the six of us tumbled out
of Thursday night, the sidewalk had wet its lips.
From the last woebegone step of the wooden front porch,
the crackling steam of sounds
trailed our next velvet act,
humming in the recount of the near-past;
the illusion of names and faces,
the blur of anecdotes coming in waves,
hammerslipping between our footsteps.
The cartoon of revelry fades as we pass
reassurance between us in lousy bottle rhythm,
We were alive just then, right? You were there.
Was I there? Am I here? What's your name?

In this hour unnamable we are no longer
cashiers and waitresses and adulterers,
no longer drunks and inventors and presidents.
The soft veneer of silhouettes dots out foot by foot
as everything about the night slowly disappears.
Different moment, the conversation continues.

I am alone and loose from history.
I hold my memory to my ear,
it sounds like the ocean.

I did not grow up just to live a long time.
There have been moments when I was aware
of the holiness as it was happening,
but holiness is only a threshold,
it is tangled in my purpose.
I have wasted so much time trying to pierce

that which is not there.

I walked myself home last night,
smiling at nothing
as I watched everything be exactly itself.
In a city that sleeps according to clocks.˙
I wore the self-assuredness of last light turner-offers,
as my feet said goodnight to everything
I would not de-fame with my eyes.
I walked without my body last night,
as slowly as I could,
knowing no time would pass
between your door and mine.

In this hour unnamable,
somewhere between midnight and the horn of fire,
we become each other,
shook free the thrift store puzzle of our cheap identities
to melt into landscapes.
When we said goodbye,
for a brief moment,
there was one voice.

STILLYOU

After I walked out,
I moved to a mountain with wheels
that could get up to seventy-five mph on the highway.
I tried to drive it across
everywhere that was vast and empty,
but you were there too.
We lay on the rocks
and tore ourselves as naked as they.
Our bodies moved together
like the shadows of clouds
caressing the desert.
I made you leather.
You loved me knife.
The bellies of those clouds made fingers
like they were trying to teach
their children about rain,
even though they had never seen it.

SINCE WE MOVED TO THE MOON

Since we moved to The Moon,
things have pretty much stayed the same.
Nobody does the dishes. There are homeless guys here too.
They steal our empties as soon as we put them out.
I don't know how they know the exact moment
we're going to put out the bottles.
I imagne the stray cat across the street is spying on us
and calling them on his walkie talkie as soon
as those plastic bins hit the concrete, the motherfucker.

One of the problems with living on The Moon
is that we don't have any furniture.
In our first week we replaced furniture with roller hockey,
but we would get tired, falling asleep in motion,
and roll off the surface of the satillite.

Even when you live on The Moon,
you fall in love with your female roommates.
In fact, it's easier. There's no TV.
You spend all night, and, all night
watching the earthrise and earthset
as if the world revolved around you.

Even when you're an imaginary person,
you still have to do the dishes.
Even when you sleep in a bed of poppies
and the walls of your house are built of music,
there's still going to be some asshole cat with an eyepatch
hanging out on your front porch
trying to teach your cat to smoke cigarettes.

The thing that surprised me about The Moon is that there's wind.
I know it's impossible, but you can tell that to the vacuum.

All I know is that my magnetic field leaps into my throat
every time I see a sudden gust command a pillar of moondust,
glinting in the earthlight, chiseling a million instant statues
in the space of an endangered breath.
Breathing is dangerous on The Moon.

They told me how lonely it was going to be,
but I expected more drinking.
Not as much looking out the window.
They didn't tell me that living on the edge
of experience was going to feel so much like
being slowly forgotten.

MANY MANSIONS

When two adult men share the same bedroom,
people come to one of a handful of simple conclusions.
The word genius is almost never mentioned.
When six people live in a four-bedroom apartment,
your co-workers snark. You make soup in bulk.
Even intimate dinners are a party. The landlord
starts to call, but I fell out of romance
with the telephone years ago.

I fell out of bed September 1ˢᵗ and found
a note from Michael Jordan written on the hub cab
of a Voltzwagen Beetle. It read,

"Two thousand one was five years ago. American culture needs
to begin again. Everyone needs to stop living at the end of time.
Sincerely, Air Jordan Symbol. P.S. You need to work on your lay-up,
you don't win games without the basics."

When me and my eleven best friends
moved into a three story house,
it was not a metaphor for my body only.
The bathroom became a barbershop,
The living room is a newspaper and a radio station and a cabaret.
the kitchen is the blogosphere.
We talked loudly about all the damage
the invention of the microwave
has done as a tool of isolation,
loud enough for the satellites to hear.
We replaced our refrigerator with a cow.
Family is a group of people
that makes your individuality stronger,
it rarely has anything to do with blood.

Human is the being of distance.
We see ourselves most clearly
in moments of love and pain and madness;
when we are stranded outside of the world.
We have been making room inside our whole lives.
Human is the primate that saw the open plains
and said, "I will go there."
The space inside of my heart will always
be greater than the entrance,
so I will have to grow larger.

It is difficult to let anyone in,
but I will go there with you.
When we let others into our hearts,
space is not lost, but gained.
The room of us is growing all the time.
There will always be room for you.
In my house there are many mansions.
This is a path I chose long ago.

this book also belongs to:

Marguerite G. Ellis, Ihsan Gurdal, Julio Canas, Justin Taylor,
Meredith Rottersmann, Simone Beaubien, Casey Rocheteau, Sarah
Morgan, April Ranger, Adam Foam, Kate Lee, Morgan Ward, Shane
Donnelly, Brian Lawlor, Shane Myrbeck, Emily Shisko, Kit Wallach,
Sean Conlon, Erich Hagan, Mike McGee, Ken Arkind, Danny
Sherrard, Jon Sands, Carrie Rudzinski, Steve Subrizi, Maxwell
Kessler, Carlos Williams, Karen Finneyfrock, Jeanann Verlee, Megan
Thoma, Leonora Symczak, Michael Collins, Sam Potrykus, Iyeoka
Ivie Okoawo, Cristin O'Keefe Aptowicz, and "The Big D" Derrick
Brown.

WB 2011 LINEUP

38 BAR BLUES
New poems by CR Avery

WORKIN' MIME TO FIVE
Humor by Derrick Brown

YESTERDAY WON'T GOODBYE
New poems by Brian Ellis

THESE ARE THE BREAKS
New prose & poetry by Idris Goodwin

THE FEATHER ROOM
New poems by Anis Mojgani

LOVE IN A TIME OF ROBOT APOCALYPSE
New poems by David Perez

THE UNDISPUTED GREATEST WRITER OF ALL TIME
New poems by Beau Sia

SUNSET AT THE TEMPLE OF OLIVES
New poems by Paul Suntup

GENTLEMAN PRACTICE
New poems by Buddy Wakefield

HOW TO SEDUCE A WHITE BOY IN TEN EASY STEPS
New poems by Laura Yes Yes

THE NEW CLEAN
New poems by Jon Sands

BRING DOWN THE CHANDELIERS
New poems by Tara Hardy

WRITE ABOUT AN EMPTY BIRDCAGE
New poems by Elaina M. Ellis

REASONS TO LEAVE THE SLAUGHTER
New poems by Ben Clark

OTHER WRITE BLOODY BOOKS

EVERYTHING IS EVERYTHING (2010)
New poems by Cristin O'Keefe Aptowicz

DEAR FUTURE BOYFRIEND (2010)
A Write Bloody reissue of Cristin O'Keefe Aptowicz's first book of poetry

HOT TEEN SLUT (2010)
A Write Bloody reissue of Cristin O'Keefe Aptowicz's second book of poetry
about her time writing for porn

WORKING CLASS REPRESENT (2010)
A Write Bloody reissue of Cristin O'Keefe Aptowicz's third book of poetry

OH, TERRIBLE YOUTH (2010)
A Write Bloody reissue of Cristin O'Keefe Aptowicz's fourth book of poetry
about her terrible youth

CATACOMB CONFETTI (2010)
New poems by Josh Boyd

THE BONES BELOW (2010)
New poems by Sierra DeMulder

CEREMONY FOR THE CHOKING GHOST (2010)
New poems by Karen Finneyfrock

MILES OF HALLELUJAH (2010)
New poems by Rob "Ratpack Slim" Sturma

RACING HUMMINGBIRDS (2010)
New poems by Jeanann Verlee

YOU BELONG EVERYWHERE (2010)
Road memoir and how-to guide for travelling artists

LEARN THEN BURN (2010)
Anthology of poems for the classroom. Edited by Tim Stafford and Derrick Brown.

STEVE ABEE, GREAT BALLS OF FLOWERS (2009)
New poems by Steve Abee

SCANDALABRA (2009)
New poetry compilation by Derrick Brown

DON'T SMELL THE FLOSS (2009)
New Short Fiction Pieces By Matty Byloos

THE LAST TIME AS WE ARE (2009)
New poems by Taylor Mali

IN SEARCH OF MIDNIGHT: THE MIKE MCGEE HANDBOOK OF AWESOME (2009)
New poems by Mike McGee

ANIMAL BALLISTICS (2009)
New poems by Sarah Morgan

CAST YOUR EYES LIKE RIVERSTONES INTO THE EXQUISITE DARK (2009)
New poems by Danny Sherrard

SPIKING THE SUCKER PUNCH (2009)
New poems by Robbie Q. Telfer

THE GOOD THINGS ABOUT AMERICA (2009)
An illustrated, un-cynical look at our American Landscape. Various authors.
Edited by Kevin Staniec and Derrick Brown

THE ELEPHANT ENGINE HIGH DIVE REVIVAL (2009)
Anthology

THE CONSTANT VELOCITY OF TRAINS (2008)
New poems by Lea C. Deschenes

HEAVY LEAD BIRDSONG (2008)
New poems by Ryler Dustin

UNCONTROLLED EXPERIMENTS IN FREEDOM (2008)
New poems by Brian Ellis

POLE DANCING TO GOSPEL HYMNS (2008)
Poems by Andrea Gibson

CITY OF INSOMNIA (2008)
New poems by Victor D. Infante

WHAT IT IS, WHAT IT IS (2008)
Graphic Art Prose Concept book by Maust of Cold War Kids and author Paul Maziar

OVER THE ANVIL WE STRETCH (2008)
New poems by Anis Mojgani

WRITEBLOODY
QUALITY AMERICAN BOOKS

PULL YOUR BOOKS UP BY THEIR BOOTSTRAPS

Write Bloody Publishing distributes and promotes great books of fiction, poetry and art every year. We are an independent press dedicated to quality literature and book design, with an office in Long Beach, CA.

Our employees are authors and artists so we call ourselves a family. Our design team comes from all over America: modern painters, photographers and rock album designers create book covers we're proud to be judged by.

We publish and promote 8-12 tour-savvy authors per year. We are grass-roots, D.I.Y., bootstrap believers. Pull up a good book and join the family. Support independent authors, artists and presses.

Visit us online:
WRITEBLOODY.COM

at citizens
who are Not capitalize
just can capitulate to
highered interest rates

in the shadows
of the banks thrown shade
at the tenants
who cannot capitalize,
just capitulate,
to their highered interest rates

If you were not entirely
in debacles, what do you
expect of anything?

CPSIA information can be obtained at www.ICGtesting.com
Printed in the USA
268683BV00001B/22/P